THE MAGIC BUS
LOST IN THE SOLAR SYSTEM

By Joanna Cole   **Illustrated by Bruce Degen**

Kingfisher Books

The author and illustrator wish to thank
Dr Donna L. Gresh, Centre for Radar Astronomy
at Stanford University, for her assistance
in preparing this book.

The author also thanks John Stoke,
Astronomical Writer/Producer
at the American Museum-Hayden Planetarium,
for his helpful advice.

Kingfisher Books, Grisewood & Dempsey Ltd,
Elsley House, 24–30 Great Titchfield Street,
London W1P 7AD

First published in this edition in the UK
in 1991 by Kingfisher Books
Published by arrangement with SCHOLASTIC INC.

BRITISH LIBRARY CATALOGUING IN PUBLICATION DATA
Cole, Joanna, 1944–
Lost in the solar system.
1. Solar system
I. Title   II. Degen, Bruce   III. Series
523.2

ISBN 0 86272 790 1

Printed in Spain

To Virginia and Bob McBride J.C.

For Chris, queen of the
Biscadorian Mother ship B.D.

WHAT IS THE
SOLAR SYSTEM?
by John

The solar system is the Sun and all the bodies that orbit around it — the nine planets, their moons, the asteroids (chunks of rock) and comets (balls of ice and dust).

It was field trip day again for Ms Frizzle's class. Everyone was excited. We were going to the planetarium to see a sky show about the solar system.

CLASS, AN ORBIT IS THE PATH OF A PLANET OR OTHER OBJECT AROUND THE SUN.

SUN

ORBIT

AL. EINSTEIN
E = mc²
MY FAVOURITE THEORIST

ALFALFA
MY FAVOURITE SPROUT

We tried to be nice to Janet.
We really did.
As we got on the school bus,
we told her that Ms Frizzle
is the weirdest teacher in school.
But Janet wasn't interested.
She wanted to tell us about herself.

As usual, it took a while to get the old
bus started.
But finally we were on our way.
As we were driving, Ms Frizzle
told us all about how the Earth
spins like a top as it moves in its orbit.
It was just a short drive to the planetarium,
but Ms Frizzle talked fast.

WHAT MAKES NIGHT
AND DAY?
by Phoebe
The spinning of the
Earth makes night and
day.
When one side of the
Earth faces the Sun
it is daytime on that side.
When that side turns
away from the Sun,
it is night.

THIS BUS IS
A WRECK.

AT LEAST IT
STARTED THIS
TIME.

WE HAVE NEW
SCHOOL BUSES
AT OUR SCHOOL.

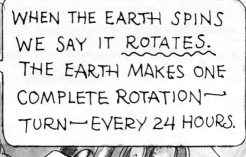

WHEN THE EARTH SPINS
WE SAY IT ROTATES.
THE EARTH MAKES ONE
COMPLETE ROTATION—
TURN—EVERY 24 HOURS.

When we got to the planetarium,
it was closed for repairs.
"Class, this means we'll
have to return to school,"
said the Friz.
We were so disappointed!

On the way back,
as we were waiting at a red light,
something amazing happened.
The bus started tilting back,
and we heard the roar of rockets.
"Oh, dear," said Ms Frizzle.
"We seem to be blasting off!"

The Friz said our first stop
would be the Moon.
We got off the bus and looked around.
There was no air, no water,
no sign of life.
All we saw were dust and rock
and lots and lots of craters.
Ms Frizzle said the craters were
formed millions of years ago
when the Moon was hit by meteorites.
Meteorites are falling chunks
of rock and metal.

It was fun on the Moon.
We wanted to play,
but Ms Frizzle said it was time to go.
So we got back on the bus.
"We'll start with the Sun,
the centre of the solar system,"
said the Friz, and we blasted off.

WHAT MAKES THE MOON SHINE? by Rachel
The Moon does not make any light of its own. The moonlight we see from Earth is really light from the sun. It hits the Moon and bounces off, the way light is reflected from a mirror.

LOOK HOW HIGH WE CAN JUMP!

I WAS IN A NATIONAL SKIPPING CONTEST. I WON, OF COURSE.

IS THERE A NATIONAL BRAGGING CONTEST?

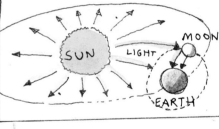

THE MOON'S ORBIT by Amanda Jane
The Moon travels in orbit around the Earth, just as the Earth travels around the Sun.

THE SUN IS A STAR
by Carmen
Our Sun is an average star like the ones we see in the night sky.

We zoomed towards the Sun, the biggest, brightest, and hottest object in the solar system.
Jets of super-hot gases shot out at us from the surface.
Thank goodness Ms Frizzle didn't get *too* close!

WHICH STAR DO WE SEE ONLY IN THE DAYTIME?

THAT'S EASY: THE SUN.

YOU SHOULD NEVER LOOK DIRECTLY AT THE SUN, CHILDREN. IT CAN DAMAGE YOUR EYES!

YOU SHOULD NEVER DRIVE A BUS DIRECTLY INTO THE SUN, EITHER!

HOW BIG IS THE SUN?
by Gregory
Our sun measures more than a million kilometres across. More than one million Earths could fit inside it!

HOT!

SOLAR FLARES are giant storms on the Sun's surface.

...and pulled away.
"We'll be seeing all the planets
in order, class," explained Frizzie.
"Mercury is the first planet,
the closest to the Sun."

MY SCHOOL IS HEATED WITH <u>SOLAR</u> ENERGY.

I HAVE A <u>SUN</u> DECK.

I HAVE TEN PAIRS OF <u>SUNGLASSES</u>.

GIVE US A BREAK, JANET.

SUNSPOTS
are areas
that are cooler
than the rest
of the Sun.

Our Path So Far

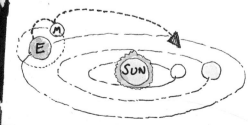

WHY IS IT SO HOT ON VENUS?
by Ralph

Venus's atmosphere has a lot of carbon dioxide gas in it. Carbon dioxide acts like a blanket to hold heat in.

CLOUDS
HEAT HEAT HEAT

When heat is trapped like this by a planet's atmosphere, it is called the "greenhouse effect".

Below the clouds, Venus was as dry as a desert.
The ground was covered with rocks.
And it was HOT!
It was about 400 degrees Centigrade!
That's *much* hotter than an oven baking biscuits!

THERE'S NO LIFE ON VENUS, CLASS.

IT'S TOO HOT!

IT'S TOO DRY!

THERE'S TOO MUCH ACID!

LET'S LEAVE!

The air was so heavy
we could feel it pressing down on us!
Ms Frizzle said there might be volcanoes
around, too.
We said, "Let's get out of here!"
"Our next stop is Mars,
the red planet, fourth from the Sun,"
announced the Friz.
"On our way, we'll be passing through
the orbit of Earth, the third planet."
The bus lifted off with a roar.

IT NEVER RAINS
ON VENUS
by Dorothy Ann
Venus's clouds
never make rain
because it is too hot
for rain to form. Any
liquid on Venus dries
up instantly.

I'VE BEEN TO MARS
LOTS OF TIMES.

JUST
IGNORE HER.

Our Path So Far

WHY AREN'T MARS'S
MOONS ROUND?
by John
Large moons are
round because of
their gravity. Millions
of years ago, when
large moons formed,
their gravity pulled
in their material evenly
and made them round.
The moons of Mars
are so small that

they don't have
enough gravity
to be round.

As we came close to Mars,
we passed its two moons,
which are called Phobos and Deimos.
Compared to our Moon,
they were tiny.
And they weren't even round!

Phobos
(29 km long)

Deimos
(14.5 km long)

Volcano

LONG AGO, THERE
MAY HAVE BEEN
WATER IN THOSE
CHANNELS,

YES, BUT TODAY
ALL MARS'S WATER
IS FROZEN IN
THE POLAR
ICE CAPS.

THOSE ARE
MOONS?

THEY LOOK LIKE
POTATOES
WITH CRATERS.

Looking down, we saw a huge canyon.
Ms Frizzle said it would stretch from
London to New York, if it were on Earth.
There was a volcano
more than twice as high
as the highest volcano on Earth.
And all around, there were channels
that looked like dried-up river beds.

WHY IS MARS RED?
by Arnold
Mars looks red because there is a lot of rusty iron in its soil.
The sky looks pinkish because of red dust in the air.

We landed and started walking around.
Suddenly a huge dust storm blew up.
Ms Frizzle said dust storms on Mars
can last for months.
They may cover the whole planet.
We scrambled back on the bus
and made our escape!

"Mars is the last of what we call
the inner planets!"
Ms Frizzle shouted above the roar of the rockets.
"We will now be going
through the asteroid belt
to the outer planets!"

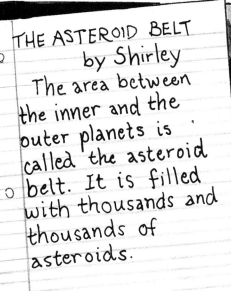

THE ASTEROID BELT
by Shirley
The area between the inner and the outer planets is called the asteroid belt. It is filled with thousands and thousands of asteroids.

WHAT ARE ASTEROIDS?
by Florrie
Asteroids are chunks of rock and metal in orbit around the Sun.
Scientists think they are the building blocks of a planet that never formed.

Thousands of asteroids were spinning all around us.
All at once, we heard the tinkling of broken glass.
One of our tail-lights had been hit by an asteroid.
Ms Frizzle put the bus on autopilot and went out to take a look.
She kept on talking about asteroids over the bus radio.

THE LARGEST ASTEROID IS ONLY ⅓ THE SIZE OF OUR MOON. MOST ASTEROIDS ARE THE SIZE OF HOUSES OR SMALLER.

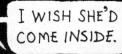

I WISH SHE'D COME INSIDE.

Suddenly there was a snap.
Ms Frizzle's tether line had broken!
Without warning,
the rockets fired up,
and the bus zoomed away!
The autopilot was malfunctioning.

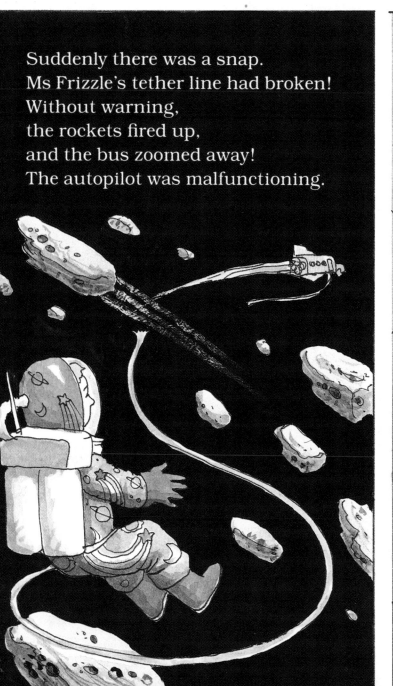

On the radio, Ms Frizzle's voice grew
fainter and fainter.
Then she was gone.
We were on our own!
We were lost in the solar system!

Most of us were too scared to move.
But Janet started searching the bus.
In the glove compartment
she found Ms Frizzle's lesson book.
As she began reading from it,
a huge planet came into view.
"Class, this is Jupiter," Janet read.
"It's the first of the outer planets,
and the largest planet in the solar system."

The next sight made us forget our troubles.
It was Saturn, a gas planet like Jupiter.
It had swirling clouds and lots of moons.
But the most incredible thing about Saturn
was its rings.
It was the most beautiful planet
in the solar system!

Next was Uranus, a blue-green gas planet
with faint grey rings and moons.
Some scientists think they might be
made of chunks of graphite –
the material used in pencils on Earth.

The bus was going faster and faster,
and we couldn't control the autopilot.
We swept past stormy Neptune,
another blue-green planet – eighth from the Sun.
All we could think about
was finding Ms Frizzle!

HOW LONG IS A YEAR?
by Tim

A year is the time it takes for a planet to go all around the sun. Neptune and Uranus are so far away from the sun that they have very long years.

One year on Uranus is 84 Earth years.

Neptune's year is 165 Earth years.

"Neptune is the last of the giant gas planets."

WE'RE ALMOST OUT OF GAS OURSELVES!

Great Dark Spot

AND THE NEAREST SERVICE STATION IS 4,000 MILLION KILOMETRES AWAY.

YOUR WEIGHT AND FATE ON NEPTUNE

Kg.	Kg
39	44
Earth Weight	Neptune Weight

You will have a happy birthday 165 years from now.

IS PLUTO A REAL PLANET?
by Wanda
Some scientists think Pluto was once a moon of Neptune. It may have escaped from the orbit around Neptune. Then it became a real planet in orbit around the Sun. Pluto was the last planet discovered in the known Solar System.

YOUR WEIGHT AND FATE ON PLUTO

Kg. 39 Earth Weight
Kg. 0.5 Pluto Weight

You will meet a small, dark, planet.

CHARON

PLUTO

We were going so fast,
we almost missed seeing the ninth planet,
tiny Pluto,* and its moon, Charon.
We were so far away from the Sun that it
didn't look big any more.
It just looked like a very bright star.
We were leaving the solar system.

*Every 248 years, Neptune's orbit is further out than Pluto's. Then Neptune is the ninth planet. But most of the time, Pluto is the ninth planet from the Sun.

THERE'S NOTHING OUT THERE — BUT STARS.

MAYBE THERE'S A TENTH PLANET WAITING TO BE DISCOVERED.

IT'LL HAVE TO WAIT.

I HOPE MS FRIZZLE IS WAITING, TOO.

Janet flipped rapidly
through Ms Frizzle's book.
Suddenly she found something new –
the instructions for the autopilot.
We punched in ASTEROID BELT
on the control panel.
Slowly the bus turned around.
It was working! We were going back!

JANET REALLY SAVED THE DAY.

I TOLD YOU SHE'S A GOOD KID.

BEYOND PLUTO:
STARS AND MORE STAR
by Alex

Beyond our solar system are millions and millions of stars. There are so many stars and they are so far away that our minds cannot even imagine it.

Some of those stars may have planets, and some of those

planets could have life on them, just like our earth.

Our Path so far

Asteroid Belt

With Frizzie back at the wheel,
the bus headed straight for Earth.
We re-entered the atmosphere,
landed with a thump,
and looked around.

BOYS AND GIRLS, WE ARE ARRIVING ON EARTH, THE THIRD PLANET FROM THE SUN.

THUMP

We were in the school car park again.
The rockets were gone.
The space suits were gone.
The bus was a wreck.
Everything was back to normal.

THANK GOODNESS!

HELLO AGAIN, OLD FRIEND.

OUR PLANET CHART

PLANET	HOW BIG ACROSS	HOW LONG ONE ROTATION (DAY AND NIGHT)	HOW LONG ONE YEAR	HOW FAR FROM THE SUN	HOW MANY MOONS	HOW MANY RINGS
MERCURY	4,850 km.	59 days	88 days	58 million km.	None	None
VENUS	12,140 km.	244 days	224 days	108 million km.	None	None
EARTH	12,756 km.	23.56 hours	365.25 days	150 million km.	1	None
MARS	6,790 km.	24.37 hours	687 days	228 million km.	2	None
JUPITER	142,600 km.	9.50 hours	11.9 Earth years	778 million km.	at least 16	2
SATURN	120,200 km.	10.14 hours	29.5 Earth years	1,427 million km.	at least 17	Many
URANUS	49,000 km.	11 hours	84 Earth years	2,870 million km.	at least 15	10
NEPTUNE	50,000 km	15.48 hours	164.8 Earth years	4,497 million km.	8	4
PLUTO	about 3,000 km.	153 hours	247.7 Earth years	5,900 million km.	1	None

In the classroom,
we made a terrific
chart of the planets
and a mobile of the solar system.

OUR SOLAR SYSTEM

Sun

⑧ Neptune
⑥ Saturn
Asteroid Belt
③ Earth
① Mercury
② Venus
④ Mars
⑤ Jupiter
⑦ Uranus
⑨ Pluto

YOUR WEIGHT AND FATE ON EARTH

Kg.
39
Earth Weight

HOW ABOUT
THAT?
I WEIGH 39
KILOGRAMS.

There's no
place like
home.

At last, it was time to go home.
It had been a typical day
in Ms Frizzle's class.
Now we had only one problem.
Would anyone ever believe us
when we told about our trip?

ATTENTION, READERS!

DO NOT ATTEMPT THIS TRIP ON YOUR OWN SCHOOL BUS!

Three reasons why not:

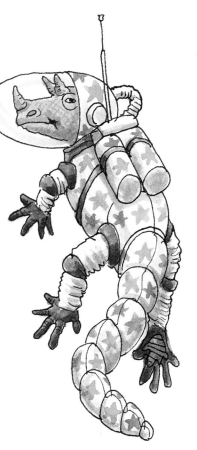

1. Attaching rockets to the school bus will upset your teacher, the school head teacher, and your parents. It will not get you into orbit anyway. An ordinary bus cannot travel in outer space, and you cannot become astronauts without years of training.

2. Landing on certain planets may be dangerous to your health. Even astronauts cannot visit Venus (it's too hot), Mercury (it's too close to the Sun), or Jupiter (its gravity would crush human beings). People cannot fly to the Sun, either. Its gravity and heat would be too strong.

3. Space travel could make you miss tea with your family . . . for the rest of your childhood. Even if a school bus *could* go to outer space, it could never travel through the entire solar system in one day. It took *years* for the Voyager space probes to do that.

ON THE OTHER HAND . . .

If a red-haired teacher in a funny dress shows up at your school — start packing!